I0465853

Without money, make yourself a billionaire

The hidden codes of success

By Ashkan . Ka

2019

if you were born poor, it's not your fault.

but if you die poor, it's your fault.

Bill Gates

Preface:

I speak in this book to you of all my secrets, that I used every single one of them to get rich and get what I am. In every word, I will tell you the secret of getting rich. how to save yourself and those around you from poverty.

I don't intend to advertise or deceive you. It's just the result of my long - time struggle, which I have long worked out between books and websites and economists and great writers, and I'm trying to help all people who 've been living through a hard life like this.

Well, if you bought this book for fun, don't waste your time, for this book can't be a good joke, because it's a key to success. But if you are the one with great aspirations, you don't know the way to get it, and poverty makes your life dark and desperate to seek a way out of poverty or you 're a successful human looking for bigger success and sweet dreams, I recommend looking at every word of this book more deeply because every word of this book gives you a key to open the doors of success. Be with us on the journey to success.

A little bit about me:

I am a son living in the richest country in the world, but I live with the poorest people. I'm a genetic expert. Perhaps in the country many of you will have a good job with a good income, but in our country, many people like me are unemployed and homeless.

I lived in a family deprived of all the possibilities of life. I hoped from childhood that I could be a useful human to the family and the people around me. I was the one who wanted to. Eventually, I was able to save myself and my family and get to life we`d always dreamed of.

It may not be easy for you, and it will be hard for you to take a lot of wealth without having a father without a free hand and in the way of achieving success from the books and guidance of successful people.

I know that poverty and hardship destroy men and their desires. I compiled this book so that I could give all the people who were desperate to get rich in the spot and seek a solution to get rich and save themselves, and in the dark looking for a light to find a way for success.

Don`t forget to know All of the words in this book, maybe you will find a way to find success among those letters.

Most of the ways and issues created in this book are by great economists and writers, and I have collected some of them that I have benefited by and helped me to achieve my goal. Perhaps I have a small share in your success.

psychology to attract wealth

Have you ever wondered why people lag behind in achieving progress and improving their financial position and a comfortable life?

The answer to this question is generally focused on the fact that financial success is impossible as long as most people create the innumerable barriers that the dam is making.

If you put up limiting beliefs about money in your subconscious, it would be difficult to get out of the narrow fence of poverty and lack of money, because your subconscious mind will eliminate all your options to earn money. For that reason, most people always think about their lives that they can never get rich. However, there are also those who believe in their fortunes, but they do not know how to achieve it.

Some people in their conscious consciousness think they can do anything to achieve their goals, but the unconscious part of their brain does not believe in their success; So the more the person follows the unconscious part of his brain, the more obstacles emerge in his daily life.

That's what the mind does. To illustrate the point, I point to an example: There are many people who, despite the use of useful books on becoming wealthy, taking part in many seminars, and using a lot of emphasis, are still grappling with a lot of material difficulties. While these people have done all the things that have been done in this regard, they are still trapped in a sort of limiting belief. They usually have different beliefs about achieving wealth.

For example:

* I don't have enough money to reach my goals in life.

* It's too late for me, I don't think I can find money.

* prices will fall in case of investment in the stock market.

* Economy is a very complex issue.

All these beliefs create barriers that trouble us to achieve wealth.

These types of thoughts limit people because they seek answers outside themselves, while the key to treasure and wealth lies in their homes. Being rich and self - sufficient is in people's minds.

Many people who are successful in the financial field often have positive beliefs about well – being. When people find out how to walk in the path of happiness, they come out of the realm of causes, and the question makes their minds self - conscious." Is it possible?"

They then review their goals and get one among them. Yes, they succeed because they have the idea of getting rich.

So instead of focusing on little things, it's best to think about why we don't have enough wealth in life. Having a proper pattern reduces the constraints on the way of success.

Once you have an idea in a better state of mind, and get away from tensions, anxiety and anger, it will be easier for you to make progress in life. The first step to help a person is to discover the nature of his problems. For example, one may have a family who has lived in poverty; so the person in his ego has the belief that he has to always be involved in financial problems, because his parents have been in such a condition; or his parents constantly remind him that he is incapable of building a comfortable life for himself.

It usually happens to children that in the early years of their lives, poverty and lack of money have a role in their mind. That kind of beliefs in "N.L.P" is called "stamp", the same stamp and role in the minds of children will make them believe in their poverty and lack of money by the end of their lives. Therefore, recognizing limited beliefs is the first fundamental step.

Once you become aware of the roles and beliefs of your subconscious, you can use the different "N.L.P" methods to remove barriers, and allow yourself to enjoy opportunities to access wealth.

What is to be done?

First of all, think carefully about your desires and ways of achieving them. Ask yourself: How can I succeed?

Now, do something different. Think about what you don't have in life.

Then, ask yourself why you don't have these things and how you can achieve them. Even with the memory of one of your dreams and aspirations, you feel good. This feeling arises because, in this case, all of your conscious and unconscious frames spread about wealth and prosperity. It may seem strange how a person can change their beliefs about these possibilities? Most of the time, people are looking for immediate results. The changes may initially be insignificant, but they are learning to think in a new way, and in this case many open doors can be seen in front of them.

We take an example to illustrate the above:

many years ago, a number of Vietnamese emigrated to the United States. Most American people were dissatisfied that the government provided them with facilities and services. But the remarkable thing was that most of the Vietnamese who entered the business world had a remarkable success, why?

Perhaps the obvious reason for that was that Vietnamese people came from a country where they had a very little chance to make up for it if they were wrong. But they came to the U.S.A, a country where the worst possible case was that no one wanted to call them on the phone or blame them for not paying a bill. finally, after migrating to America, they lived in two or three families under a roof, and by doing difficult and low - income jobs, they saved the money, and in a short time they made a business with the money, and all the family members in addition developed the trade. As a result, there was no need to hire the workforce. So, after a while with profits from the business, they bought property and went on to buy more real estate.

There was success, proof, and emphasis on the possibilities as everything was possible for them. To achieve their long - term goals, they were buying a short - term pain and hardship. So it`s a way of wanting success.

If you have come from a point in the world that death awaits you at any moment, be grateful and happy for being alive instead of anger and frustration, and ask yourself this question rather than frustration and bad, and ask yourself: Is success possible?

patience is a blessing

For most Germans, saving money is customary for buying large and expensive items and paying cash. In Germany alone, there are only people who have people, their rent, or the debt to buy their cars. After buying their goods, they immediately start saving to buy their next goods.

They don't even grieve for a moment to put their money back on their intended purchase; therefore, instead of wasting their energy on how they achieve their goal, they wait patiently for their purpose.

The ability to delay gratification is the topic of Dr. Daniel Goleman`s book entitled "emotional insight". In this book, the author concludes: Those who can wait and endure to reach their demands are on the verge of success.

Real self – sufficient

Most people worry about their incomes. Either one person earns $ 1 million a year, or fifteen thousand dollars; in both cases there is a desire to earn more money, and people are never satisfied with their incomes.

During the Nazi regime, there were countless wealthy people in Germany who were sent to forced labour camps after their property was confiscated. "Viktor E. Frankl" and "Ann Frankl" though they were in the worst condition of life and poverty but they still had a rich and rich life.

Victor Frankel in his book entitled "Man`s Search for Meaning," he believes that only one thing can never be taken from man, and that is his vision and insight into life.

He says: We have lived in a forced labour camp, we can remember people going to the others ' huts and giving them comfort and giving them the last piece of their pie. Although the number of those people was very low, it is enough to prove that everything can be taken from human beings, but one thing cannot be taken and that is the last human freedom in choosing its behavior in any circumstances.

Frankl, as a psychologist, admitted his creative attitude that helped him out of the tough conditions of life in a forced labour camp.

Is money a measure of human value?

As we noted above, Viktor E. Frankl lost all his possessions, even his shoes, and the only thing left for him was his ability to believe and admit that he was still a good man, despite everything from him.

This view is invaluable because it proves that having money and wealth in a long period cannot be a criterion to value itself, it does not determine who you are, but just a source, what is important is having confidence in your confidence. The money is just an external factor. When people feel better about themselves, they fear less failure. Today the price is measured by spending money; the more you spend, the more you value yourself.

Now I point to an example: Consider a woman who has inherited $ 17 million from her parents. He spends at least $ 800,000 to buy his favorite stuff, for example, in a shopping mall It costs about 180,000 dollars to buy clothes and shoes, but all this is because of Jealousy with her sister. The sister, who had inherited the same amount, would make much of the same. But he does not look at money as an aspect of his identity, and he did not consider spending as a sign of value. She began a successful business woman, so that during the course of a few years the profits of her business were several times her original assets. But the sister who had the money to value herself was soon lost all of her money and went bankrupt.

Therefore, those who do not put their identity and value on the basis of external factors are soon tired and frustrated. When a person loses judgment and judgment about himself and others, he begins to notice great changes in his life as he sees life from the window of his eyes, and others do not take the opportunity to recognize themselves. Rather than seeing the pros and cons, this person focuses on his abilities and points, trying to strengthen the positive aspects of his being and eliminate the negative aspects.

So with our better understanding, we can achieve the source of happiness that is going on within us. This understanding will help us to understand the outside world, and as a result we will solve the obstacles and problems of our way easier, and we will achieve what we dream of in life, including having a life full of comfort and comfort.

The golden rules of getting rich

Have you ever wondered who the millionaires are and how they become millionaires?

If we do not consider corruption, there is usually a legal form of two ways to become millionaires. One benefit from the benefits of the rich father and the death of the "harrowing" and "untimely" father is rich and the other having ideas and persistence.

millionaires like other humans have their "individuality". But can one also find common points? Like the same habits that are the pattern of their lives? And what features are these millionaires who are famous for self - made people?

There are golden rules that prove to you that getting rich is your right, and no one can take that right away from you. You have only to know and believe them, so you can enjoy the wealth you have earned.

Every time, everyone asked you, "The wealth is better or anything else" you can say, without any shyness or inward conflict to protect your image, say wealth. Allow me to say that you have the right to do so, and do not hinder it.

No one gets rich in good luck and no one with bad luck would lose their money. This suggests that becoming rich as well as achieving any other demands in this world has its own stages, and only those who are aware of this issue can hope for their wealth.

You know that no one has gotten anywhere without trying to get anywhere, even the easiest work and the easiest thing in the first place begins with a lot of work and effort.

The first secret most important is trying. We must not stop trying at all times so that we can reach the destination we want.

To be rich, you have to try. Whether you like to be wealthy is different from what you really want to be wealthy. With luck you can`t get financial independence. You must do your best to achieve financial independence.

Do not forget that without try, there will be no success. If you want to get rich, you have to endure the hardships.

Usually, people who do not have a great goal will end their efforts with the slightest difficulty, but if you can handle the hardships, you will soon reach your goal. Note that all those who succeed in life may face difficulties at the start and will have to resort to a frustrating attempt.

You have to deal with difficulties so you can reach your goal. When Thomas Edison decided to invent the bulb, he did not succeed in making his first attempt. He decided to come to his dream and, despite being defeated more than a thousand times, stood so hard until he succeeded.

Know the value of your money and do not let your money dominate you. You are the master and the king of your money.

Know the value of your money and do not spend it in vain. Most people do not have control over the type of money they spend and without any thought they spend without paying attention. If you want to be rich, you need to know when and where to spend money. In no school or college do not teach the principles of wealth. You get these principles only through traveling in the community and studying and researching the lives of the wealthiest people in the world. To be able to control the amount of financial assets in your life, you need to know the best way to use your money. Try to use the experiences of others and do not commit the mistakes they committed.

Have you ever thought for whatever reason you spend money?

1. You spend it
2. you save it
3. you invest it
4. Or that he gave his money in a good way.

The question you may ask yourself is how can you spend money creatively, that is, you spend well and save well?

To answer this question, first of all, you need to specify how you spend. For some, spending money is a kind of fun, some also spend money on gesture.

Some people have addiction to spending money. If you want to become wealthy, you must be the master of your money.

Having a goal to be rich is a very important issue. To achieve success, you have to have a goal and try to reach it. If you want to get $ 1 million in wealth, you have to try as much as 1 million dollars. The most important step in achieving wealth is a principled and practical application. The goal you consider for yourself should be accessible. You should not be planning financial planning with closed eyes and with no prior planning and considering all the conditions of action. For instance, as long as you have a lot of debts, you must not decide to save money. Your first plan should be to clear your debts.

Are millionaires born from the first rich to the world? If your answer to this question is no, why do you not get rich?

One of the secrets of millionaires in most of the world's richest people is to save money. Another important thing in the way to get rich is to save money. If you want to achieve your desired wealth, you need to know what other ways the others have used, you are bound to use the same principles in your personal life, depending on your situation. There is no specific limit to saving, but it is not confined to money specifically. You can even save time and use the hours you get by saving time to increase your income. Saving is a shortcut to reach wealth. The more you can save, the better you can keep your money from spending your money. The amount of savings has nothing to do with the amount of your income. There are many ways to save money, you must consciously save.

Before you make a decision to save money, you have to know the right meaning. Some people make mistakes in saving money. By doing so, they deprive themselves and their families of the simplest pleasures, and thus deprive their families of joy and comfort. The condition of success in saving money is an understanding about it with your Spouse.

Helping others on your way to your goal can be very helpful. By helping other people, you can also foster your spirits and your heart, you can also get big things and big ideas like entrepreneurship.

The view of the rich in the lives

We talked about how we should be able to get rich, but let's think about how the rich are looking into life. Your way of thinking is vital to acquiring wealth; But today we know that without the use of beliefs and beliefs designed to generate wealth, we can never achieve any fortune. It is the basic ideas that separate the wealthy from other people of society.

The first step begins to capture wealth from basic beliefs that form in the mind.

I don't mean that if you create these beliefs and ideas in your mind, you can easily become a billionaire, or get any kind of wealth you dream about, because action, effort and persistence are essential to the money to get rich.

For our efforts to lead to wealth, we need a firm foundation that first appears in the human mind.

What is the view of the rich to failure?

Billionaires and other rich people don't look at failure as a game that has ended forever. They look at failure as a temporary barrier to achieve success and an opportunity to learn. All the wealthy have been failed several times on the way to their desired wealth, but they always consider failure as an opportunity to learn that helps to reach their dreams and goals.

Henry Ford, in the best possible way, summed up the case:

The local defeat is for rest. A chance to start again but more wisely than before.

They will never surrender. All the rich benefit from such perseverance, which is more like a maddening obsession. But we must not forget that this is the extraordinary vision that has brought them to the place they are. They commit to achieving their goals and never give up until they reach all their goals and dreams.

Steve Jobs says of resistance and perseverance:

I believe that half of what makes successful entrepreneurs separate from unsuccessful entrepreneurs is sheer resistance and persistence.

Another thing that separates the ordinary people from wealthy people is the kind of thinking. The rich, the great think and the great dreams. They don't limit themselves to small dreams.

If you have no great dreams, you can never achieve it. It's as simple as that. If you want to be a billionaire, you have to have a long vision and work hard and clever to turn your dreams into reality.

Donald Trump says:

I love great thought. If you want to think about anything, think big.

They have a strong mind about money and wealth. As I said before, your attitude about wealth is the basis of wealth. Everyone who is rich today has a unique and strong mind about wealth. They have deeply believed that being rich is a good thing. They were comfortable with money. They have even been comfortable with spending. In fact, they loved wealth. If you do not have a true and powerful view of money and wealth, you can never earn a lot of money.

The rich believe that they are ruling their fate and they themselves are writing their destiny.

Billionaires believe that using a set of right thoughts that are supported by extensive and appropriate action, they can create a clear and prosperous future.

It is one of the big differences of the rich with the common people who think they have no control over their lives and should only be open to realities of life.

Another important issue is to take responsibility for our work and not make our mistakes to other's neck.

Successful people assume responsibility for their results, whether positive or negative.

Even when they fail and face complicated obstacles, they still claim responsibility because they love it and know that by accepting responsibility they send the message back to their minds that they have the power to change the negative results and not give up until they achieve success.

It doesn't matter to achieve the goal of security. Security and avoidance of danger have no place in the life of a successful human. They enter the money's game from the beginning to win.

Will you do the same?

Please do not take a mistake. The rich never Gambling with their money, but when the opportunities are placed on them, they don't lose the opportunity by thinking about losing their property or maintaining what they have, but they always seek to find ways to get rich. because they realize that there is a lot of wealth in every corner of this world. It is only when they create a unique value in other's lives, they can gain huge wealth.

In this world, as much as all human beings, there is enough wealth.

The belief of the rich in general is in contradiction with the belief of ordinary people thinking that money is hard to earn and to get rich.

The rich know and believe that the IQ and their education have nothing to do with money and Earn wealth.

Money flows into the pockets of people who find opportunities and create value, and all the billionaires also know that this is the only way to earn wealth.

They know the market determines where wealth is going, and if you use this opportunity at the right time and place, the flow of wealth will flow to your bank account.

Another issue is that if you can help people in solving a particular problem and do this on a large scale, you can easily generate more wealth. The billionaires know and believe that if you can help a lot of people to meet their desires, you can easily accumulate a great deal of wealth.

Zig Ziglar summarizes this in the best possible way:

"You can get everything you want to achieve in life, only if you want to help a lot of people to get what they want."

We know that the rich are unique people. All of the wealthy, millionaires and billionaires in the world benefit from these shared insights on money and wealth, but unfortunately, ordinary people do not have these beliefs.

Although having these insights alone can`t make you rich in life, but they can surely be a spark in your mind and a start to start earning wealth, and it's the fact that it will create differences.

Ultimately, this is what you need to change your financial condition.

3 important decisions in financial life

Now is the best time to review three decisions that will undoubtedly change your financial life.

There is nothing worse that a rich person is always upset and angry.

There is no reason for this, but yet I am dealing with this phenomenon every day. This is due to unbalanced lives and high expectations, as well as dissatisfaction with individual attitudes.

You can't achieve your true desires without appreciating what you have.

But how to balance in life? What does it mean in an unbalanced life of success?

At any given moment, people make 3 key decisions that will lead their lives.

If you do not accumulate caution when making these decisions, like most people, you are physically not in a good position. They are emotionally depressed and worse and economically in stressful situations. But if you make a conscious decision, you can change the your way of life today.

First decision: Choose the topic you care about carefully

At any given moment, millions of issues compete for your attention.

You can think of things that are happening right now or next to you, or things that are going to happen in the future. You may also think of the past. Everything that you notice is sent to that energy. The topics that matter to you and how it works is shaping your whole life.

What is your focus on what area? Do you focus on what you have or things that are not in your life?

I'm sure you pay attention to both coins.

You may need to admit that you need to be grateful about issues other than economic ones;

You can be proud of your health, family, friends, situations and mind.

No matter what you disabilities and defects you have, The important thing is how you can succeed despite these defects, In that case, you are no longer incomplete.

The imperfect meaning is not to have any physical or mental disability. The imperfect is the one who can`t find a way to save himself and succeed in his path in any circumstances.

Raise your accolade habit of gratitude can bring a new level of health and emotional wealth to you.

Find the secondary consideration pattern that affects the quality of your life; do you focus more on things that you can control or vice versa?

If you notice things that you can't control, you add more stress to your life. You can influence many aspects of your life, but you can't control them.

When you get this focus pattern, your brain is ready for the second decision.

Second decision: check what all these things are for?

Your way of thinking about your life has nothing to do with the accidents and economic conditions or situations that happen to you. By being worth or worthless these issues in your life will determine the quality of your life.

Most of the time, you do not know the role of your subconscious mind in meaningful life events.

When something happens (like an accident, illness, loss of job), do you see it as a beginning or an end? If someone is against you, does he insult you, train you or really worry about you? Is a destructive problem meant to be negative? Or perhaps you have received a gift from God?

Your life is based on the meaning that you have given it. Every meaning creates unique emotions, and the quality of your life involves a place where you live emotionally.

There are always this question in seminars:

How many of you know some peoples who they consume on antidepressants but they are still depressed?

Typically, 85 - 90 % of the participants raise their hands.

How is it possible? The medicine needs to improve people!!!

But the truth is that, according on the label of antidepressant pills, one of the side effects may be thought of suicide.

But it doesn't matter how much medicine a person consumes. If he constantly cares about things that he can't control or doesn't have, he can easily get frustrated.

However, if that person finds a new meaning for life or a reason to live or believe that everything is going to exist, he continues his way with a lot more power than before. When people change their usual habits and meaning of life, there will be no restrictions on the change of life. Changing the focus on life can actually change the nature of his life in a few minutes.

Therefore, take control and remember that life is equal to emotions and feelings equal to life. Be alert and open - minded. In any event, you will find a powerful meaning and thus riches in the deepest meaning of life will be made available to you.

When you make a sense of meaning in your mind, emotions emerge in you, and those emotions will cause a mood to realize the third decision.

The third decision: What will you do?

Your emotional state strongly affects your actions. If you are angry, you have different behaviour to when You feel a lot of liveliness.

If you want to shape your actions, the fastest way is to change your focus point and set the meaning of your life on a stronger issue. Two angry people behave differently. Some retreat and some move forward.

Some people are expressing their anger more calmly. But others they show it very loud and violent. Some others are looking for a situation in order to show their passive aggression or even take revenge.

Where have these behavioral patterns come from?

The human tends to shape his behavior like persons his respected and loved ones. How do people who make you tired or angry? You usually take they are approach away from yourself. You see, however, that you have selected patterns that you have seen over and over when you are young and you did not like it. It's very good that you know about your patterns in times of frustration, anger, discomfort, and loneliness. If you don't recognize them, you will not be able to vary.

Now that you have mastered the power of these three decisions, look for patterns that they are experiencing what you want of life. I promise you that those who have an optimal relationship will focus on completely different issues than those who always fight, and have a completely different meaning for the challenges involved in the relationship.

This is not rocket launcher science. If you are aware of the differences between the people's approach to these three decisions, you will have a way of making positive changes in every area of your life. Especially in the realm of finances on the paths of acquiring wealth.

10 management principles for acquiring wealth

Rich people manage their money differently than others. They make different decisions and have a completely different view about money. But even if you 're not rich, you can manage your money. There are 10 practical methods that the rich will manage their money differently than anyone else.

1. Delay the joys

Humans tend to behave differently in the face of the pleasures of life. We all love those joys. This behavior has come about in our distant past. When you 're trying to get rich, the desire to take immediate pleasure doesn't help you in this direction, but it will hurt you. You'd better hold the balance and think about the decisions you take and think about the size of your current expenses and think about your future wealth.

2. Understand the difference between wants and needs

Maybe you tell "we need a bigger house". Don't let your wants and needs cause your confusion. A common mistake among the poor is that they justify their demands as the need for themselves. Then they get a poor financial decision and even feel better. The rich know the difference between what they want and what they need. So distinguish this distinction and do not fool yourself.

3. Automatically invest

There are many ways to automate the investment, such as an automated deduction of the salary and investment in the pension fund, which is a good way, but it is more important to think about investing. Whether it is automatic or not, the riches will deeply believe that they have to do it normally, such as brushing each morning. Do not ask how much they invest, they know how much they need to invest as their goal has already been established and they know how much money they need to invest in order to achieve their goals.

Roy Shepherd, millionaire, and financial adviser says:

"Save 15 per cent of your income for your future."

Working with this principle is very good to start.

4.Understand the concept of debt

how much is the monthly repayment? This is what the poor people ask when they buy a car. It's the wrong question. The better question is, " How much does the car really cost me?"

When you multiply the monthly reimbursement in the number of months, it gives you a shocking number that is higher than the car's value, and you have not yet included depreciation, tax and other expenses. This is a figure you must deal with. But you would not better come along with your old car!

5.Start with a goal

Know what you want and what you need to do to achieve it. If you don't know what you are looking for, you find out what is the result of a series of decisions taken to enjoy the fleeting pleasure of life, which eventually leads to heavy costs and financial poverty. Decide how you want to live, choose a true target, then estimate how much it will cost you and do things that will help you reach the specified point.

John Simon, 28, a millionaire on real estate business, says:

"What kind of life do you want at retirement? Estimate the amount you need, then work with a specific strategy to reach that amount."

6.Live at a moderate level than your income

An important issue with automatic investment (Principle 3) is that the wealthy may spend below their average level. If you start your investment as soon as possible and more than the amount you need to reach your goal, you can use the remainder for daily expenses.

The important thing is that, with your savings priority, you can`t afford to spend more than it`s left, and therefore you spend less than your income.

I emphasize again: spend less than your income.

7.Make short - term sacrifices

Think larger than you have in your mind. Think what your current decisions will affect your future. The whole story of getting rich is that you have more than you want. But sometimes you need to sacrifice the current demand for something more, bigger and better in the future. So, bigger than you want now to think.

8.Ask for Help

Follow your expertise and give financial management to consultants and professionals. Focus on the value your investments make in this world. However, you have to know about money management. Understand at least the basic concepts of economics to understand the financial adviser's statements. This information can easily be achieved. The rich have written numerous books in this regard.

The millionaire entrepreneur, vladimir jendelman says:

"I know how to grow and develop businesses, but I give my financial management to professional financial consultants."

9.Learn to calculate

I don't talk about geometry and trigonometry. It's just arithmetic, subtraction, and simple split. The riches study numbers when making a decision. Ordinary people, for example, believe they better buy a new car so they don't spend a lot of money on their vehicle when their vehicle is quickly ruined. That's not necessarily true. By spending a great amount of money you can fix your car and still be more affordable than the new car. Think about all the calculate of buying a new car.

10. Use your opportunities

Use when you have a good opportunity to invest in. By identifying the market that is profitable and using (Principle 9) that is to calculate the expected profit and loss, enter the market in terms of risk and value. The opportunities are rare, so be prepared and act on time.

It is easy to manage money in the way of the rich, and it's not hard at all. If you want to get rich, manage your money using these 10 principles.

You may sometimes have to sacrifice small things in the short - term, learn new information and work hard to save money to invest money. Your work is a very happy result and you can do great things in this world and attain some inner satisfaction, which is the true demand of everyone in the world.

If you can` t apply all this 10, just remember this key point: spend less than your income.

How can we be an Independent millionaire?

Millionaire or billionaire in the life of today has become a wish that can only be seen in the photos ... as if in real life such a great life could not have happened, but this view is completely wrong.

It is quite possible to make a billionaire, and for your convenience, there is nothing to do with the circumstances of the country, the circumstances of your family and even your initial capital.

In this section, we examine 10 signs that you are on the right track to be a millionaire, even if you don't feel it yourself.

1. You have set great and valuable goals for yourself

You may had heard this beautiful sentence saying: Take the moon, even if you`re not in the moon, you`ll land among the stars.

If your personality is in a way that you need a '80' Score in a lesson, but you only think of a score of 100 and you will not to less than that be satisfied with it, you have to be proud of yourself because your mindset is just like the mindset of the millionaire and the wealthy.

In your mission to reach a wealth of 1 billion or even $ 10 billion, choose the target, not $ 1 or 2 million. Go on with introspection, and use the magic of the great think to achieve financial security.

2. You have a mind open to different ideas

You are not afraid of new ideas, and you know that a closed mind can never inspire confidence, courage, conviction, and imagination. Self - made millionaires change their attitudes towards the category of wealth, success, and happiness.

3. Use your time to obtain beneficial results

You understand the fact that time is much more valuable than money and wealth. Because you want to focus your time and energy on tasks that you have great skill to do, you prefer to hire people to help you complete your tasks and responsibilities that you don't have much expertise or experience to do.

Individuals who use every moment and opportunity to get more results and opportunities to gain more results and success and go where they feel they are winning, not just working and completing the tasks.

4.You enjoy targeting and achieving goals and success

If you 're passionate about the Scoping Phase and achieving your goals, you should know that you think like millionaires.

Peter Voogd, founder of the Game Changer's Academy, who earned his first one million in dollars before the age of 26. he said:

"You can't accidentally get a million dollars, if it isn't one of your goals and you can never get it."

5.In the face of hardships and problems, you are optimistic, choosing a positive attitude

Many self - made millionaires, including J.K. Rowling has experienced poverty -reaching wealth in the real sense.

J.K. Rowling was a lonely mother who lived with the benefits of state-owned interests and by using all his talents and capabilities and concentrating all his attention, he tried to reach targets and demands that were more important to him than anything else.

Rich people believe: "I shall make my life"

The poor people believe: "Life is only an accident"

6.You are fully aware of the events and events that occur around the world around you

If your personality is such that instead of starting your day with Facebook and other non - essential tasks, you 're doing your most important tasks at the beginning of the day or, according to brian trascy, in the book of "Eat that Frog", If you swallow your biggest and ugly frog at the beginning of the morning, I congratulate you because one of the habits of rich people is in your life.

Successful entrepreneurs like Bill Gates and, Warren Buffett their day start with the study of famous news publications to the Wall Street Journal, and the New York Times,

7.Being poor is meaningless to you

If you deliberately delete all your excuses and beliefs that try to make you poor to be poor, you are on the way to success.

Bill Gates says:

"if you were born poor, it's not your fault. but if you die poor, it's your fault"

8.You work with a successful instructor or are looking for such a person

You must understand that you must not limit yourself to the ideas of the defeated people.

If you study the story and lifestyle of your self - made millionaires, and you know the benefit from a professional coach as one of the main tasks of personal and occupational success, you 're going to take another step toward becoming a billionaire.

68 percent of the 400 Americans listed on the Forbes Magazine's 2013 billionaire list were self-made billionaires, the heirs of the wealth of nobody else, and there was no windfall in them.

Very likely, the majority of such self - made billionaires have benefited from a highly educated mentor who taught them the right way to think outside the common thinking framework in society properly.

It does not matter if that coach is in person, or articles and books from economists.

9.Avoid bad debts that make no progress

Do not use debt that does not create any money and wealth for you, make it one of the laws of your life.

If you borrow money to buy a car, this should ensure your income increase. While the rich use debts as an effective investment lever to grow their cash streams, the poor use debts to buy things that make the wealthy richer.

In almost all his books, Robert Kiyosaki has defined the concept of bad debts and good debt as follows:

Good debt puts money in your pocket, and bad debt will be taken out of your pocket.

10.You save for investment

You know, the only reasonable reason you save money is that you want to invest it. Save some of your monthly income in a safe and inaccessible bank account. Never use the money saved in this account for anything, not even the necessary items, as this gives you pressure to increase your income, which is critical. Invest in excess of your money in paper assets and other types of assets, such as property and business creation.

Work for Yourself

Surely you do not think that you can get rich from work for others??!!

You may be able to use working for others to pave the way for your goal and save money that you get from work in those places, or by putting yourself in the workplace to get a bit of the way to start your effort, but you can never achieve the wealth you aspire to.

When you work for someone else, you are helping her get rich and become more powerful every day, but you, who spend hours of life in this, earn a steady and basic salary without any progress every year. Now he wants it to be administrative or free and in the market.

If you want to set a goal for your success, one of the first steps is to be independent and work for yourself.

When you have a job that own yourself, you can concentrate on it with your taste and economic thinking, starting it from zero and reaching where your goal is.

The biggest incentive for someone trying to succeed is to know the more you try, all the benefits and damage that comes to you are all just for you, and it can be the biggest incentive to know that everything is just for you and more, and you can have more than one fixed salary.

The goal you make is quite dependent on you and your interests.

Everyone has talent and everyone is interested in a particular job, a person in music, someone in the investment, a person in the construction, everyone in every field has talent and interest, if he is trying for them, he will succeed.

No matter what your goal is. Once you have an interest in it and feel that you have talent in it, it is the biggest factor to succeed in that purpose.

You can be a travelling salesman but with that same job, you can reach power and wealth, if you act with interest and talent and creativity.

No matter what your career is, achieving success has seven great secrets, which is preferable to all the things said:

1.Trying, 2. Interest, 3. Perseverance, 4. Creativity,

5. Proper saving, 6. To be independent, 7. Wait

A little about my job

Maybe I need to talk a bit about my job and the way I used it to achieve the goal and success.

I was always interested in two jobs, the first of them genetics I chose as academic discipline, hoping that someday I might be able to work in this field, but there was no job for a genetic expert in my country, and there was needed a lot of funding to establish a genetic institution, and since there are no helps for entrepreneurs in my country, so I couldn't even be independent. For this reason, after graduation, I temporarily abandoned this wish.

But I did not withdraw, and did so much research, so that I could find in my second interest, a great path to earn a fortune.

The Forex and Binary Option were methods that helped me to reach the goal.

Yes, one of the hardest and risky businesses in terms of investment and economy. It wasn`t important to me to be risky, because I always had a lot of interest in the stock and investment so I tried for success.

At first I had no expertise about them. Their training courses were expensive, and because I had to go to another city for them, it was hard to be successful. But I did not retreat, I was working for about two years in food shops. I saved part of the salary I got, and paid the rest of my salary to buy train tickets, and pay tuition fees.

At first, I failed several times. I lost a lot of my money first, but I wouldn't give up. I had no right to fall back, because I had the big ambitions and intentions in my head.

I learned something new from every failure. Every failure showed me a corner of the mistakes and the wrong strategies I had, and every time I persuaded me to read and try to rectify my mistake.

yes, i was able to succeed. Those seven laws really answered.

If you do not strive to achieve wealth, it's your fault, not your country, neither your country's economic policies nor anyone else's, just and only that's your fault.

So you do not have the right to make someone else responsible for your problems. Neither your father nor your mother or anyone else is responsible for your poverty and problems.

They just cause their own problems and poverty.

So, if you are poor, it is your fault that you sit down, and you don't try.

And if you 're trying, but you could not get a success, Of course, seven rules of success have not been fully complied with.

It's never too late to try and fight. No matter what age you have, be sure you can.

I told you everything that helped me all this way, and shared everything I'd experienced across the path and shared with you all the things that I learned from the elders of the economy and the successful people.

Those who are interested in Forex and Binary Option and want to be on track with me to achieve the goals that they have. Please and thousands of please research as many as possible and enter the field with knowledge.

90 % of those who enter Forex or Binary Option have failed miserably and are only 10 % of them who win.

It is ten percent of those that spent the days of months, and even years, to learn and learn the science of the profession.

In this job, you can double or even multiply the amount of money you invest in 24 hours if you are carefully researched and knows the best way to invest in it.

If you go without information and science and invest with closed eyes, make sure you lose all your assets in less than an hour.

There is no concern for learning and spending Forex and Binary Option training courses.

Learning is much easier today, and you can get all the training and tools necessary for a good and accurate investment for free or at very low prices from the internet.

But no one will tell you the secret of success in this way.

It`s just you who have to find the path of success with great effort and training.

Six important steps to turn a wish into wealth

(Think and Grow Rich) written by Napoleon Hill can be found among the best books in history on the subject of wealth and the secrets of getting rich.

Maybe we need to give a brief overview of this great book so that we can more easily talk with you about ways to reach wealth so that it's easier to understand the way forward.

It is one of the books that everyone has to read during his lifetime.

It is interesting to know that Napoleon Hill was not a writer or researcher. He was just a simple journalist.

Hill went to Andrew Carnegie to do one of his interviews. Carnegie saw Hill's seriousness and determination. For this reason, he chose to teach Napoleon Hill his principles of success. Carnegie's teachings are within the core of the book "Think and Grow Rich". This book can be one of the greatest help and tips to keep you on track of success.

There are thousands of books on financial success on the shelf of libraries and they all recommend that you spend less, save more, make a better investment, retire sooner, get rid of debt sooner, and they solve all of the financial puzzles in the same subject, where in some parts to start and prepare your mind for better understanding of the number of steps you need to take, we dealt with them.

But perhaps none of the books described the issues better than the book published in 1937. Napoleon Hill, one of the most influential authors of that time, interviewed more than five hundred successful men (Americans) so far, to explore the key to their luck.

He published all of his research, in a 200-page book, titled "Think and Grow Rich", one of the best-selling books of the whole era.

he writes: "You won't get rich just with to wish, but what makes a person rich, the desire and desire to be rich and to have a perpetual thought about it, then planning a way to get rich, finally, keep track of the program with maximum diligence, so that failure is meaningless to him."

In a conclusion, he expresses the six steps to convert a wish into wealth:

1. in your mind determine the amount of money you wish to have. It's not enough to say, " I want a lot of money." Set the exact amount. (There are psychological reasons for this)

2. determine what you 're going to give in return for this amount of money. (The fact that says, " There is nothing for nothing.")

3. Make a careful date to reach your desired amount.

4. Pour a certain plan to achieve your desired amount, and if you are ready or not, start your work in practice and implement your plan.

5. Write clearly determine the amount of money you would like to get, and determine the amount of time you need to achieve that amount, write what are you going to give in order to reach that, and clearly describe how to accomplish your plan.

6. Read your writing aloud, twice a day, once before bedtime, and once in the morning. As you read, see and feel, and create the belief that you are in that position.

It looks so simple, but if you compare with any of the other rich help guides, you`ll see exactly the same steps. They only raise the issue with more noise.

The Hill`s book reminds us that one of the only ways to reach wealth is to know that most of our time emotions and mindsets is a barrier to progress, and our work is to overcome these bad feelings with a clear plan.

You read these phrases from Napoleon Hill:

(In this book, I have referred to the richness code of people, that I've been studying and interviewing for years with precision about this. I learned it from Andrew Carnegie.

Carnegie, this lovely Scottish man, asked me to deliver his words to the people of the world. I accepted his offer and, with the help of Carnegie, I stand up to this promise.

If you have been frustrated so far, if you have already been affected by a problem with your psyche, if you have tried and failed, it is the Carnegie formula that you need to understand and use in your life.

One of Carnegie's secret features is that when someone is surrounded and used, he finds himself in the path of achieving an unexpected success. To achieve success, you have to pay for it, even though this cost is so small compared to what you get.

If you are prepared to receive this passwords, you will advance half the way of success and understand the other half as soon as it comes to your mind.)

According to the author of this book, the acquisition of wealth is not out of reach, and you can get what you want. Wealth, fame, recognition, and happiness can be the share of all who have decided to achieve it.

Part of the summary of the book "Think and Grow Rich":

(In planning for wealth, do not let anyone ruin your dream. Never listen to what others said. Dreams are not like clouds in the air.

Thomas Edison wanted to build a lamp that lit up with electricity and succeeded.

The Wright brothers wanted to build a plane, and they managed to invent the plane of their dream flight.

Beethoven was deaf, and he played music.

O. Henry worked his imagination in prison, and made a great writer.

Charles Dickens, after his love failure, became one of the world's greatest writers.

Helen Keller was deaf, blind, and Mute. Despite these mischiefs, she became one of the greatest women in history.

She proved: "If someone does not consider himself a loser, among the those who have failed ones will not be."

50 years ago, medicine went to the village and sold a large kettle and a wooden mixer to the drug dealer of that village. The money that the drug dealer paid to that doctor was the total savings of his life. The drug dealer bought an idea. An old kettle, a wooden mixer, and a formula written on paper Became the product we now know as "Coca-Cola".

Consequently, if there is a will, there will many ways.

Secrets of Success According to Andrew Carnegie

In 1848, Andrew Carnegie entered the United States with much less than $ 1 in his pocket. But 53 years later, he was the richest man on earth. At the height of his power, a journalist, Napoleon Hill, who was interested in the story of his success, went to the rich man.

Mr. Carnegie saw the seriousness of Hill, and on this basis, in 1908, he decided to give him the task of registering and writing all the strategies of acquiring wealth as well as his public works.

the two together created a great deal of innovation in the genre of self-help books, "Think and Grow Rich" was later published by Napoleon Hill, in 1938, and became one of the best - selling books of all times.

When Hill was starting his career as a successful writer, Carnegie told him "his 10 success laws". These 10 laws are the foundation of most of the works of Hill. Read on a brief summary of them:

1. Determine your purpose: Make a "plan of action" and walk right along the path.

2. Make a "wonderful collection"
   Hill says, quoting Carnegie: "Connect with persons and work with them, that things you do not have, they have."

3. Try more than usual
   Hill writes: "Effort, more than what you have to do, the only thing that makes promotion, and makes people committed to you."

4. Take practical faith: Believing in yourself and your goals makes you work perfectly with confidence

5. Have an individual initiative: Without any instructions, do what is to be done.

6. Open your imagination: Give yourself courage to think beyond what has already been done in your field.

7. Show your enthusiasm: Having a positive way makes you ready to succeed and Makes others respect you.

8. Think about all the details: From view Hill, the precise thinking is " having the ability to separate the facts from the imagination and use relevant items in the interest of resolving concerns and problems."

9. Focus your effort: Don't let anything distract you from your most important task and mission that is you

10.   From your Miserable, make a profit:

Hill writes: "For each retreat in life, there is an equal leap" So you should not be disappointed with the failures.

A little bit about the wealthy of the world

In 2017, the record for the richest people on the ground broke. number of billionaires grew 13 % this year, it reached 2043.

According to Forbes, in 2016, the rich of the world was 1810, In 2017 they number of grew 13 percent. The net asset value of the wealthy rose by 18 percent to 7.67 trillion dollars. The change in the number of billionaires since the last 31 years.

Warren Buffett, the USA`s No. 2 rich, says:

"When I was 7 or 8, I had the chance to find the really favorite thing: Investment. As long as I reached 11 had read all the books related to the investment in the public library in Omaha.

My father was active in the investment area, and when I went on Saturdays to dine with him I would read his books. A few years later, when I studied at the University of Nebraska, I bought a book that made the biggest impact on my business life.

I read "The Intelligent Investor" from Benjamin Graham's book over and over again. The book is written like as philosophy, it is highly readable and is easily understood. This book gave me an investment philosophy I still use."

That was the strategy:

(Finding a good business and buying shares- The business you can find out is why it's good- and that this business has an advantage over others that can compete with them in a long way, manage by honest men, whose stock prices seem reasonable)

Do not forget that we are not going to buy the companies and sell them the next month or next year. We need something that 10 years and 20 years and 30 years later can earn money. We need a management team that we trust and admire. No one can take away the things you have learned, and all have potentials that not yet used. If you can strengthen your talents and boosting your potential to 10, 20 or 30 percent, no one can tax on it. Inflation cannot reduce its value. You will have it all your life.

The world's richest man, Bill Gates, was named among the richest men in the world for the fourth consecutive year in 2018. His assets were $ 86 billion in 2017, a rise of 9 billion dollars compared to 2016.

Mark Zuckerberg says:

"A few years after the start of Facebook, a few big companies intended to buy it and almost everyone on Facebook said it would be better to sell, but I didn't want it. I wanted to see if we could link more people together or no. This led to a serious debate in the company so that over a year everyone in the Facebook's management team left it. It was my hardest time on Facebook. I believed in what we were doing, but I was left alone. And the worst of it was my fault. It has taught me that it is not enough to have a great goal yourself, you have to make this commitment to the goal in others.

I didn't tell anyone about my dreams for Facebook. I never dreamed of establish the company on, but it was in me that I Must link people together and Facebook was the result of this feeling. Now people often ask me about launching their company, and I basically say:

Your goal should never be the launch of the company. Focus on the change you want to make in the current situation. Find people who have a common goal with you, you will eventually find the opportunity to build something it will also target others and have a positive impact on the world."

Amazon's owner, Jeff Bezos in 2017, added $ 27.6 billion to his assets, and his total assets hit 72.8 billion dollars.

He says:

"We are in middle a great transformation, where customers have found extraordinary power. Before, they said If you happy a customer, he will tell to five of his friends. Now, by a microphone in the name of the Internet, they can tell 5,000 of their friends. Previously, you could sell a low-quality product with marketing in the market. Customers now decide which product or service is good or bad. Transparency has gone very high.

Customers can compare products easily and decide. Now part of the marketing of products is done by customers. Now the product has to be really good to go for sale. It is in the interest of the client and in the interest of the companies that have adopted the new trend and it is in the interest of the community."

The United States has more billionaires than the rest of the world, recording another record with 565 wealthy people in 2017. China is ranked second with 319 richest, followed by Hong Kong, Germany and India.

Successful poor

It`s hard for many of us to realize that most the great world`s stars had a hard life one day, and they were not so successful at first. They did not eat caviar from the beginning, they did not have expensive clothes and did not own expensive houses. It's hard for many to understand that humans can persevere and strive to reach everything, and it`s not just the power of those who have rich fathers. In fact, the reality is that not all billionaire, billionaire have been born. In fact, many of them had nothing at first and lived in extreme poverty.

From poverty to wealth, it may not be more than a stereotype, but a fact that we have actually witnessed and will be. With incredible stability and persistence there were people around the world which disturbs logical equations and from nothing, they could make everything.

In this part of the book, we look at the lives of some famous and wealthy individuals who have had a tough life, they were poor, some of them were homeless and lived in the worst condition of life, but they made the dream they wanted.

In this part of the book, an answer is for all those who think There is something called "impossible". So read with open mind.

1.Arnold Schwarzenegger:

Maybe it's better to first start with my favorite star Arnold Schwarzenegger, which is one of the great Symbols in effort and perseverance.

If Arnold Schwarzenegger wasn't there, they had to make one like him. All the world knows, it can be made possible from the impossible, even if anyone does not believe you.

Mayor, filmmaker, actor, entrepreneur, investor, benevolent, and immortal symbol of the world of bodybuilding, it's only one of the few honors that was the result of the childish fantasies of an Austrian boy named Arnold Schwarzenegger.

Since his childhood, he loved to be different, as a teenager, he entered the world of physical fitness.

At the age of 15, he began the gym and won his first gold medal at the age of 20 at the Master Olympia, but it wasn`t enough to for Arnold the success of this Olympia ... he wanted more success.

For this reason, he entered the professional competition and won the Master Olympia gold medal for seven years and became the best bodybuilder in the world ... an honorary record that has not been broken to this day.

Arnold Schwarzenegger not only got a lot of titles and honors in the world of bodybuilding, but his book's encyclopedia of bodybuilding and hundreds of articles and books from him to this day are among the most important references in bodybuilding.

But when the successes of the bodybuilding world have finally satisfied Schwarzenegger, he decided to enter the world of cinema.

At first many people mocked him and rejected him. When he decided to enter the Hollywood world, he traveled from Austria to the United States and, according to himself, "with empty pockets but full of dreams ..." began his adventure.

Several directors and producer underestimated him and refused, even one of one of the most famous directors had said sarcastically" that we would call you if we had the role of a giant monster ..." but Arnold didn`t give up.

He finally won a role in "Conan The Barbarian" historical film, which brought him many awards and honors. After two years, the director of the movie world, James Cameron gave him the idea of playing the "Terminator" in which he was Shone well and his success in the movie world became more and more the next day.

After the world of Hollywood, Arnold entered politics and humanitarian work.

Many admired him, and after 70 years he published his first book of his life as "Total Recall: my unbelievably true life story".

The book was quickly bought with a large flood of readers and was reprinted several times.

2.Howard Schultz:

Schultz told the Mirror's British media:

"When I grew up, I always felt like I was living on the other side of the world, and the rest of the people I know have more resources and more money on the other side, and they 're happier. And for some reason, I don't know why and how, I wanted to cross the barrier, and I got what people said it was impossible. I may be wearing a suit and tie, but I know where I came from and I know where that is."

After graduation, Schulz began to work at Xerox, but shortly afterwards, he joined coffee shops, Starbucks. Starbucks had only 60 stores in the United States at the time.

Schultz reached the management of the entire company in 1987 and now, Starbucks has 16 thousand shops all over the world.

His net worth about 2.9 billion dollars. (Wikipedia, February 2019)

Sources: Business Insider

3.Oprah Winfrey:

Oprah`s first experience on television was not so flattering. An unrivaled lady of television was fired from her first TV show. At that time his managers told him he  was too emotional and could not control herself in front of the camera. Oprah used this feature, by earning $ 3 billion in capital, the title of the richest woman in the world.

She once at Harvard and during his transfer of experience, said:

"There is no meaning in the name of failure. Failure is one way of life to guide us to the right path."

She was born and Grew up in poverty and hardships, but became the first black Presenter in Nashville.

Oprah was born in a poor family in Mississippi, but she couldn't keep her from going to the University of Tennessee, becoming the first African American television host at the age of 19.

In 1983, Winfrey moved to Chicago to run the morning show. The show was renamed the "Oprah Winfrey Show" in September 1985.

Her net worth about 2.6 billion dollars. (Forbes, January 2019)

Sources: Business Insider

4.Jan Koum:

The Koum was born in Kiev Ukraine. At age 16, He went to California with his mother. There they managed to get an apartment with the help of the government. John sweeping
the local shops to earn a living. They had emigrated to America, and since they had no money, he had to write a plan that would make good sale, that's how WhatsApp was born.

He learned the computer skills himself. In 2009, he founded the world's largest messenger service called WhatsApp, which was bought by Facebook in 2014 for $ 22 billion.

His net worth about 9.2 billion dollars. (Forbes. August 2018.)

Sources: Business Insider

5.Ingvar Kamprad:

When Kamprad was a 7 -year-old boy and lived in Sweden around 1920, he sold matches to his neighbors.

Then he sold the greetings card, pencils and Christmas celebration jewelry.

At age 17, he founded a company called IKEA. At 21 - year - old began selling household appliances, and the story began as IKEA's imperial. Today, he producer has more than 340 large shops in 42 countries and earns a $ 36 billion per year. New Yorker, IKEA, was named the invisible designer of the family life.

At the age of 88, Kamprad continues to collide as moderate and refuses to fly with any aircraft except economic class aircraft.

His net worth about 58.7 billion dollars. (Bloomberg, January 2018)

Sources: Business Insider

6.Shahid Khan:

He is one of the richest people in the world, but when Shahid Khan came from Pakistan to the United States, he was studying the pot while at University of Illinois, he washed the dish for revenue.

His assets include the American football team Jacksonville Jaguars and the Fulham Football Club.

The Flex-N-Gate company is one of the most valuable U.S.A companies, the owner of which is Shahid Khan.

His net worth about 7 billion dollars. (Forbes, February 2019)

Sources: Business Insider

7.Michael Jordan:

One of the most enduring names of the basketball world, before achieving its successes, has experienced many failures.

He was very fond of basketball when he was in high school, but he could never get to the main school team.

In a famous comment about his achievements, Jordan says:

"I during my sports career More than 9,000 shots to kicked out. I have lost nearly 300 games. In 26 games, when I could win my own team, I wasted the blow. I have failed in my life over and over again, and that is the reason for my success."

About 60 % of the wealthy and famous people had a tough life in the past. Apart from those we mentioned, it can also be noted to Jim Carrey, Leonardo DiCaprio, and Sarah Jessica Parker also pointed out that despite the hard past, they are the successful persons today. But don't forget that these people are just a few of them.

The very important things to notice

-Some people believe in the wrong opinion of money that money can`t happiness. This idea is completely false, it will be very difficult without the money of peace and happiness. You have to try to earn money.

How many of you know about your investment and the ability to create value?

- You`ll grow to a place where your mental image lets you.

- You will succeed in believing that you are entitled to happiness, health, and wealth.

- A system will be success when that able to teach us how to build wealth and how money really works and how to run a business.

- In the end, the decision to reach wealth and success is greater than it relates to money, that is in determining the purpose, growth, and excellence. When you start this journey, occasionally remind yourself that the goal is not just to reach your destination; it is a growth and excellence in this direction.

- A successful entrepreneur will make use of every individual in a reasonable and fitting position with its capabilities.

- You have to have a logical view of your idea and business space and possibilities, otherwise when failure or not achieving the goal, you will encounter extreme mental problems a drop of confidence, and pessimism.

- The entrepreneur must prepare himself for a variety of events, for example, to insure his own employees and businesses, so that he can maintain his idea in an emergency.

- Don`t get all of your mind involved in making money. Money alone is not a goal, but you need to engage your mind in a creative activity. The rich always think about what the best possible thing is to do in any situation. When all your mind is in the right job, wealth will also come after it.

- Powerful people have high confidence. Self - confidence is the skill you can grow in yourself, and when to talk, and what exactly to say in every situation.

- Remember to be part of a team and have a specific role. Your role has a much greater impact and responsibilities, but do not bring down the value of other team members ' efforts.

The last word:

In this book We became acquainted with the ways of acquiring wealth and education, and became acquainted with the lives of people who were poor but by persistent, industrious, and wait, Became the hubs of economics, sports, and art in the world.

You probably got to an obvious conclusion:

- Success is possible for those who have no choice but to succeed.

- Ultimately, it is you who choose your way of life.

Your life begins at a time when you are empowered to control your destiny.

Cyrus the Great

www.ingramcontent.com/pod-product-compliance
Lightning Source LLC
Chambersburg PA
CBHW051335220526
45468CB00004B/1656